P9-ELV-776

Of Course I Love You

Of Course I Love You

Robert Masello

BALLANTINE BOOKS

NEW YORK

Copyright © 1993 by Robert Masello

All rights reserved under International and Pan-American Copyright Conventions.
Published in the United States by Ballantine Books, a division of Random House,
Inc., New York, and simultaneously in Canada by Random House of Canada
Limited, Toronto.

Grateful acknowledgment is made to the following for permission to reprint previously
published material:

Doubleday: Excerpt from Letters to Mamie by John S.D. Eisenhower.
Copyright © 1977, 1978 by John S.D. Eisenhower and Mercantile Safe Deposit
& Trust Company as Trustees for the Estate of Dwight D. Eisenhower. Reprinted
by permission of Doubleday, a division of Bantam Doubleday Dell Publishing
Group, Inc.

HarperCollins Publishers: Letter from E. B. White to Katharine S. White from
Letters of E. B. White. Copyright © 1976 by E. B. White. Reprinted by
permission of HarperCollins Publishers.

Alfred A. Knopf, Inc.: Excerpt from Beloved Prophet by Kahlil Gibran and
Mary Haskell, edited by Virginia Hilu. Copyright © 1972 by Alfred A. Knopf,
Inc. Reprinted by permission of the publisher.

University of Illinois Press: Excerpt from The Poet and the Dream Girl:
The Love Letters of Lilian Steichen & Carl Sandburg, edited by Margaret
Sandburg. Copyright © 1987 by the Board of Trustees of the University of Illinois.
Reprinted by permission of the publisher.

Library of Congress Catalog Card Number: 92-90481

ISBN: 0-345-38209-9

Designed by Ann Gold
Manufactured in the United States of America
First Edition: February 1993
10 9 8 7 6 5 4 3 2 1

Contents

Of Course I Love You

A Declaration
of Intent

With this book ... I thee woo.
Again, if I've already won you over.
Anew, if I'm still working at it.

With this book, I 'fess up to all my failings. Not
that I have very many. But yes, I'm sometimes
thoughtless, self-absorbed, cranky.

And with this book, I hope to convey all the
things I think and feel about you ... but that,
inarticulate brute that I am, I don't often get
around to saying.

With this book, I hope to answer the one
question you shouldn't ever have to ask.

And no, it's not where did I put the keys.

It's do I love you. Of course I do. Through
thick and thin. Come hell or high water. I knew
it the moment I met you—or at least a *very short*

time thereafter—and nothing since has changed my mind.

Okay, so we argue once in a while. Who doesn't. But don't I usually let you win?

And okay, so I don't always do my fair share around the house. I was under the impression you *liked* vacuuming, washing dishes, doing laundry. I didn't want to deprive you.

But now that I know you *want* to be deprived, okay . . . I'll start to pick up some of the slack. (Have I said this before? This time I mean it. Really.)

And all right, I'll agree to give our relationship as much time and attention as I give to my job. And to the box scores. And to my golf game.

So in short, this book represents an avowal of my love . . . and a declaration of the new man. Of course I love you. If you doubt it for even a minute, just read on. Assembled here is an entire volume of love poetry and love prose, of tender letters, sweet sentiments, and true stories of love triumphant, all designed to prove to you, once and for all, that you're the one woman for me, and I'm the one man for you. Like it or not, we were made for each other.

And I like that just fine.

Six Reasons Men Don't Say Three Simple Words

𝒩ow, you may wonder, as I'm told many women do, why men are so reluctant to say these three simple words: "I love you." If you're prepared to hold your fire, I'm prepared to tell.

Unmanliness. Any betrayal of a deep and profoundly felt emotion—aside from such laudable displays as anger and lust—is extremely suspect; boys (and what are men but boys who now wear Relaxed Fit jeans?) are taught to treat emotions like poison sumac.

Control. And boys are taught another thing, too—that to be a man is to be in, and under, control. Saying "I love you" doesn't seem like a very "controlling" thing to do . . . especially as it could easily lead to . . .

Vulnerability. What if you were to say "I love you," and the object of your affections replied,

"That's nice." What if she didn't say it back? WHAT IF SHE DIDN'T FEEL IT?

Public humiliation and scorn. What if word of this development got out? Memories of crossing the gym floor to ask a girl to dance—who then declined—are as fresh in a man's mind as this morning's shaving cut.

Commitment. If ever three little words carried the pungent aroma of responsibility and obligation, these are the ones. Surpassed, perhaps, only by "I do."

Obviousness. Many a man will argue, "Why do I have to say it? Don't you already know?" As proofs, he will offer that he's stopped dating, he's always around, he remembers your birthday—things like that. Actions, he will claim, speak louder than words.

So it falls, unfortunately, to you to remind him that although actions speak, words are nice, too.

Thus chastened, most men will fall into line. Work with them on enunciation. Stress the importance of repetition. Show them how pleased you are with each performance. Gradually, the lesson should take, and he should be able to say "I love you" without mumbling, blushing, or checking first under the sofa cushions for hidden microphones. Men may be recalcitrant—but they're not untrainable.

———

Terms of Endearment

Of course we have our own private nicknames for each other, my little chickadee, but perhaps you'd like me to employ a new one now and again. Maybe you're ready for a change of pace. Perhaps you'd just like a little variety in your life. With that in mind, I've gone to great lengths to compile the following list of endearments and tender appellations. Are there any you'd like me to use in future? Any that strike your fancy, or touch your heart? Your wish is my command, so simply check off any you'd like to hear from now on, and I'll add them instantly to our own romantic vocabulary. (And if there are some you really don't like, you can certainly let me know that, too. No use starting a fight over something as trivial as "chubby cheeks.")

But how would you feel about ...

—light of my life   —sugar
—honeybun   —cupcake
—lambchop   —turtledove
—snookums   —muffin
—sweetheart   —cutie
—darling   —snowflake
—lotus blossom   —angel
—baby   —hot lips
—kitten   —jellybean
—sweetie pie   —dearheart
—squeenie   —lovebug
—dumpling   —creampuff
—lovey   —my little cabbage
—wee bairn   —(other)

Composed around 1903, and prominently featured in something called *The Lover's Dictionary*, the list below provides an interesting glimpse of love and marriage, turn-of-the-century style. Look it over, and let me know what you think. (Shall I start wearing a hat, so I'll have something to doff whenever we meet?)

TWENTY-ONE SURE SIGNS OF TRUE LOVE IN MEN, 1903

by Max O'Rell

*M*an betrays his true love for a woman very much in the same way as a woman betrays hers for a man. I have been thinking the matter over, and I believe that the following are fairly sure signs of true love in a man towards a woman. Ladies, kindly note:

I. When, at your request, he gives up all the habits to which you object, such as gambling, drinking, the use of language too forcible, and even smoking, if you should be so tyrannical as to insist on it.

2. When the little familiarities you may allow him to take with you never cause him to forget the courtesies that a gentleman owes to a lady, either in private or in public.

3. When he seldom speaks or writes to you of his love, but constantly performs acts of devotion, thoughtfulness, and consideration. Never mind what a man says or writes, mind what he does.

4. When he prefers the home you make for him to his club.

5. When he never fails to take notice of what you wear and of the slightest changes you may have made in your coiffure or in any part of your general appearance.

6. When you know how he would like you to do your hair, though he does not breathe a word on the subject.

7. When you are wrong and he is right (this may happen), and he only turns his head away, smiles, and says not a word.

8. When he asks you to join him wherever he goes.

9. When he never reminds you of what he may have done for the love of you.

10. When he takes off his hat to you whenever he meets you.

11. When he enjoys all your little fads and in-consistencies, and indulges you in them.

12. When he likes to have you near him when he works.

13. When he does not snub you for liking things which he does not himself fancy.

14. When he rushes up to tell you first a good piece of news.

15. When he takes as much interest in your boudoir as he does in his library, his smoking-room, or any other place of his pre-dilection.

16. When he cannot enjoy the things he likes best unless you are by his side.

17. When he sees a beautiful frock on a pretty woman, and thinks that you would look much better than she in it.

18. When he is always ready to excuse your faults and shortcomings.

19. If both of you are sitting near a table on which only one lamp stands, and you are en-gaged—you in doing embroidery, and he reading the paper—when he sees that the lamp is nearer to you than to him.

20. When he is away from you and does not write to you long, affectionate letters and does not expect any from you either, but every day sends you a telegram with prepaid answer to know how you are getting on.

_____

21. A sure sign of great sympathy between a man and a woman is when they always agree in discovering in a person a likeness to one of their mutual acquaintance.

Ninety years later, some things have changed, and some things haven't. How can you tell if a man's in love with you today? I, too, have been thinking the matter over, and here are some up-to-date signs of his devotion. Ladies, kindly note:

TWENTY-ONE SURE SIGNS OF TRUE LOVE IN MEN, 1993

1. When, at your request, he hands over the TV remote-control and watches whatever you decide on (even if it's "Knots Landing").
2. When he shows not the slightest bit of worry when you play back the messages on the answering machine before he's had a chance to screen them.
3. When he takes out the garbage, re-folds the newspaper after he's done with it, and puts the toilet seat down, without your having to ask.
4. When he prefers the home you make for him to the Happy Hour at Bennigan's.
5. When he smooches up a storm with you at home, and holds your hand when you walk through the mall.

6. When he pages through your *Victoria's Secret* catalogue, and then actually orders something for you from it.

7. When he can't wait to see you wearing what he ordered.

8. When he invites you to come along on his fishing trip—and doesn't look too stunned when you take him up on it.

9. When he stops to ask for directions when you point out to him that you're lost.

10. When he seems genuinely unperturbed if you beat him at something—checkers, tennis, Scrabble—even if it's in front of living witnesses.

11. When he doesn't gloat if he does win.

12. When he's willing to admit that, yes, he too really wanted Rocky and Adrienne to find each other at the end of the movie.

13. When he's not ashamed to confess that he's afraid of spiders, doctors, and a tax audit.

14. When he never turns to check out another woman on the street unless he's absolutely sure you're not aware of it.

15. When, if he *is* caught checking out another woman on the street, he's man enough to admit that yes, he was looking at her . . . but it's only because he thought it was someone he used to work with.

16. When he keeps you informed, in mind-numbing detail, of what's going on at his job—

even if you never have been able to keep all the players straight.

17. When he not only listens to what you have to say about your own job, but actually asks a question that shows he was paying attention.

18. When he welcomes your mother, your sister, your friends, to the house ... and then makes himself scarce so you can enjoy yourselves.

19. When he never uses his power-saw before 8 A.M.

20. When he never fails to notice if you're wearing a new outfit ... but doesn't even ask what it cost.

21. When he still gets jealous if your old boyfriend shows up at your high-school reunion.

Love Stories—
Real Men . . .
Expressing Real Feelings

"I am English. Kathy, my wife, is American. According to her, we met on line to a movie. I saw things very differently; as far as I'm concerned we met in the queue for a film. So even there, right at the very start, there was for me something different about her, and something very complicated about us. We met in England, that much we agree on, and although we only had a few weeks before she returned to New York, by the time she left I knew that I had met someone who in some way would remain a part of my life. In the five years we courted across three thousand miles there is one thing above all that kept me in love—her voice. More than our letters, it was the timbre of her voice that enchanted me. It had a musical quality and a soft warmth that embraced me in a way that no photograph could do. It was breathy, but it also lilted with a hint of Irish burr. Often it sounded nervous, as if expecting the worst, but it responded to my tongue-tied English reserve with such generosity of love that I would come away from the phone under a spell, the sound of her carried with me for days. Now that we have been truly together for almost a decade and our love for each other is much more complicated, I still remember how it was her voice which sustained me when there was little else, and how unexpected are the ways in which our lives are so utterly changed."

Chris, 35, art dealer.
Married four years.

"Our first date set the tone for our entire relationship. We went to a movie about hockey. No, it wasn't *Love Story*, the romantic weeper starring Ali McGraw and Ryan O'Neal. It was *Slapshot*, a Paul Newman romp about life in the minor leagues. As soon as she saw me waiting for her outside the theater, she laughed at my shorty short raincoat (it was never seen in public again). Then we laughed at the movie, and later at the bar I laughed at the inadvertently suggestive way she drank Labatts beer out of a bottle (she later told me it wasn't inadvertent).

That was fourteen years ago. Now we have a baby son who thinks it's a hoot to spray food out of his mouth. I think he'll fit in nicely."

David, 38, author.
Married twelve years.

"When did I know it was serious with Denise? The first weekend we spent together. We were just a few weeks into the relationship, and it was one of those lazy Sunday afternoons. I was lying around in bed, watching the NCAA basketball championships and reading the paper during the commercials. I remember, one of the sports columnists had written that only an idiot preferred sex to college basketball, and I'd laughed out loud. Denise asked me what it was I was laughing at, and when I told her, she didn't crack a smile or anything. She just looked at me, perfectly straight-faced, and said 'We can always make love once the game is over.' A woman who understood that sex and sports can co-exist—that's when I knew just how big this relationship could be."

Rick, 40, lawyer.
Married ten years.

"I know that most people think of blind dates as kind of a joke, but that's how I met my wife.

"A woman I worked with said she had this friend, who was really attractive but was dating nothing but losers. I remember saying, 'And that's why you thought of me?' And she said, 'No, of course not—I thought you could change her luck.' I was very suspicious—women are always claiming their friends are really attractive—but I wasn't doing so well myself at that point, and I thought, what the hell. I agreed to meet her in the lobby of a nice hotel near where I work—she told me she'd be wearing a blue dress with white swirls—and I can still see the whole scene like it was yesterday: she came through this revolving door, looking around for me, and I was so surprised at what she looked like that it took me a few seconds to get up off the sofa and introduce myself. She was beautiful—still is—but what I remember best was her shoulder. The way the dress was made, it uncovered one shoulder, and all the time we were having drinks in the hotel bar all I wanted to do was lean across the table and bite that shoulder. I was mesmerized. I tried to get her to go to dinner with me afterward, but she said she had another appointment, so I had to just walk her outside and flag a cab. Later on, I found out she hadn't had another appointment at all, but she just didn't want me to think she was going to be that easy. The funny thing is, she still likes to play games like that—never letting me take her for granted or anything—and I honestly think it's part of what's kept our marriage as exciting as it is."

Hal, 51, systems analyst.
Married sixteen years.

"I first met Linda—or maybe I should say I first spotted her—in a Baptist church, deep in the heart of New Jersey farm country. I was attending for the first time (a new and strange experience for me), along with some friends. After taking a seat in the second pew, I watched as the choir filed into the front loft, and I picked her out immediately. She stood out like a wild flower amidst the crops—her shining red-blonde hair a crown of glory among the ordinary heads of grain. I didn't meet her at that time, and the next time I attended church I swear I saw her with another guy (though to this day Linda claims she still can't figure out who it could have been). We finally did meet several months later, in the parking lot, when the church was dedicating a new sanctuary. But I can honestly say, it was love at first sight, from that moment I caught a glimpse of her, quietly filing into the choir loft."

James, 40, pastor.
Married seventeen years.

"Betsy and I grew up in the same hometown, and I'm not sure that there was ever a time when I wasn't secretly in love with her. On summer days, when I'd ride my bike past her house, I'd hear her practicing the piano—and I'd lean the bike against a tree, and lie down on her front lawn to listen. Other times, I'd take a detour through the halls of our high school just on the chance I'd bump into her leaving a classroom. Once I reviewed a play she was in for the high school newspaper, and thoroughly compromised my professional credentials by mentioning virtually no other performer in the entire review. We actually did go out on a date every now and then, but I was always so nervous it would have been better if we hadn't; the first time I tried to kiss her in the front seat of my mother's car, I actually slipped right past her and wound up kissing the inside door handle—and then, of course, I had to act like I hadn't just done the stupidest thing in my life. Today, Betsy's married to a guy she met at work—a real straight arrow, from what I hear— and I'm seeing a couple of different women, but no one special at the moment. Still, I sometimes wonder what would have happened if I'd ever done a better job of pressing my case ... if, after kissing that door handle, for instance, I'd gone ahead and kissed Betsy, too."

Phil, 25, stand-up comic.

The Languages of Love

*R*ecognizing the strange but awesome power of foreign tongues, I have assembled here a kind of United Nations of love. There isn't a single phrase or declaration to which I do not sub-scribe—though I can't say there's many I could pronounce. To enhance your enjoyment, and to make some sense of all this, translations have been helpfully provided.

If you'd really like me to recite these, I sup-pose I could give it a shot.

But wouldn't you really rather preserve the mood and read them silently to yourself?

In Italian

*M*adre del Dio! Quanto ti voglio; voglio man-
giarti, voglio rosicchiare i tuoi orecchi! Le mie dita
hanno il prurito di pizzicare tuo culo generoso—il
quale curva da pesca, saldo come una mela! Mi
impazzisci! mi fai diventare un barbaro! mi fai vol-
ere lasciare la moglie!

Translation

*M*other of God, how I would like to eat you
up! How I would like to nibble on your earlobes!
How my fingers itch to pinch your generous bot-
tom—round as a peach, firm as an apple! You
make me crazy! you make me wild! you make me
want to leave my wife!

In German

Ach du lieber, mein schones Rheinmädchen,
kann ich dich nicht verlocken, bei mir in dem
Biergarten, unter den linden, zu sitzen, um ein
himmlisches Bier, zu trinken oder veilleicht einen
Strudel, zu geniessen wahrend du dich in meinen
breiten Lederhosenschoss kuschelst? Und sag
mir—was hältst du von meinem neuen Tiroler-
hut?

Translation

Oh, my darling, my lovely Rhine maiden, can I
not entice you into joining me here under the linden trees of the beer garden, to quaff a stein of
heavenly brew, or enjoy perhaps a piece of strudel,
while nestling in my ample lederhosened lap? And
tell me—what do you think of my brand-new
badger bristle hat?

In French

*A*vec ces yeux, ma chère Fifi, je t'adore! Avec
ces bras, je t'embrasse! Avec ces doigts de pied, je
te fais rire! Tu m'apparaît plus belle que La Nôtre
Dame au clair de la lune, que la Seine à l'aube,
que Paris au printemps! Je te couvre avec de gros
bisous, ma biche!

Translation

*W*ith these eyes, my darling Fifi, I adore you!
With these arms, I embrace you! With these toes,
I tickle you! You are more beautiful to me than
Notre Dame by moonlight, than the Seine at
dawn, than Paris in springtime! I cover you with
kisses, my little muffin!

In Spanish

¡Por tí, escalaría las montañas más altas de los Pirineos! ¡Por tí, cantaría las canciones más tristes bajo tu ventana! ¡Por tí, llegaría a ser torero para poder brindarte las orejas!

Translation

For you, I would scale the highest peak in the Pyrenees! I would sing to you, beneath your window, sad love songs on my guitar! For you, I would gladly brave the bullring at high noon, and award you the ears of my conquest!

Lighting the Fire

(Pointers on Pursuit and Desire)

If the heart of a man is deprest with cares,
The mist is dispell'd when a woman appears.

John Gay,
The Beggar's Opera (1728)

Caresses, expressions of one sort or another, are
necessary to the life of the affections as leaves are
to the life of a tree. If they are wholly restrained
love will die at the roots.

Nathaniel Hawthorne

And what is bettre than wisdoome? Womman.
And what is bettre than a good womman?
Nothyng.

Geoffrey Chaucer
"The Tale of Melibee"

"I positively adore Miss Dombey;—I—I am perfectly sore with loving her."

Charles Dickens,
Dombey and Son

Love is the greatest refreshment in life.

Pablo Picasso

Beauty to no complexion is confined,
Is of all colours, and by none defined.

George Granville

Love, and a Cough, cannot be hid.

George Herbert
Jacula Prudentum

My heart, the bird of the wilderness,
has found its sky in your eyes.

Sir Rabindranath Tagore
The Gardener

Whilst Adam slept, Eve from his side arose:
Strange his first sleep would be his last repose.

Anonymous

*L*ove in its essence is spiritual fire.

> Emanuel Swedenborg
> *True Christian Religion*

*L*ove is an ocean of emotions, entirely surrounded by expenses.

> *Lord Thomas Robert Dewar*

A beauty is a woman you notice; a charmer is one who notices you.

> *Adlai E. Stevenson*

*A*merican women expect to find in their husbands a perfection that English women only hope to find in their butlers.

> *W. Somerset Maugham*

*L*ove does not begin and end the way we seem to think it does. Love is a battle, love is a war; love is a growing up.

> *James Baldwin*

The supply of good women far exceeds that of the men who deserve them.

Robert Graves

When a man, for instance, is attached to a woman because of her outward harmonious appearance, i.e., beauty, it means that she pleases his sense of sight. If he is fascinated by her beautiful voice, then his sense of hearing has been appealed to. When he falls in love by the touch of her soft little hand, then his tactile sense has been excited. The meaning of all such attachments is the desire to satisfy the senses. Hence the love is sensual. For any of the five senses may be the starting point of sexual desire.

Bernard S. Talmey, M.D.
Love: A Treatise on the Science of Sex-Attraction (1919)

In his younger days a man dreams of possessing the heart of the woman whom he loves; later, the feeling that he possesses the heart of a woman may be enough to make him fall in love with her.

Marcel Proust
Remembrance of Things Past

$\mathcal{T}$he female woman is one of the greatest insti-
tooshuns of which this land can boste.

Charles Farrar Browne, aka Artemus Ward
Woman's Rights (1862)

$\mathcal{M}$usic and women I cannot but give way to,
whatever my business is.

Samuel Pepys
Diary (1665–1666)

$\mathcal{I}$ could wish that we might procreate like trees,
without conjunction; or that there were any way
to perpetuate the world without this trivial and
vulgar way of coition; it is the foolishest act a
wise man commits in his whole life, nor is there
anything that will deject his cold imagination
more, when he shall consider what an odde and
unworthy piece of folly he hath committed.

Sir Thomas Browne
Religio Medici (1642)

I was in love with a beautiful blonde once—she drove me to drink—'tis the one thing I'm indebted to her for.

W. C. Fields

*I*f a young man is in a small boat on a choppy sea along with his affianced bride and both are seasick, and if the sick swain can forget his own anguish in the happiness of holding the fair one's head when she is at her worst—then he is in love.

Samuel Butler
The Way of All Flesh (1903)

A man fell in love with a woman who resided in the street of the tanners. If she had not lived there, he would never have entered this evil-smelling section; but since she dwelt there, the street seemed to him like the street of the perfumers.

The Zohar

The Stamp of Approval

(Loving Letters Men Have Penned)

Maybe I'm not the model correspondent. There's just something about writing a letter that puts me off. Maybe it's the telephone; it's so much easier. And a postcard hardly seem worth the trouble; even when I fill it out, I can't ever find anyplace to buy a stamp until I get home again. And then it really seems pointless to mail it.

Still, other men before me have surmounted these difficulties, and actually managed to send their sweeties countless missives, filled with tender sentiments, beautifully expressed. Here, direct from Cupid's own epistolary files, are some of the most touching and memorable examples I could find.

Let me tell you, some of these guys really knew how to work a mailbox.

From Napoleon to Josephine

Verona, November 13th, 1796

I don't love you, not at all; on the contrary, I detest you—You're a naughty, gawky, foolish Cinderella. You never write me; you don't love your husband; you know what pleasure your letters give him, and yet you haven't written him six lines, dashed off casually!

What do you do all day, Madam? What is the affair so important as to leave you no time to write to your devoted lover? What affection stifles and puts to one side the love, the tender and constant love you promised him? Of what sort can be that marvelous being, that new lover who absorbs every moment, tyrannizes over your days, and prevents your giving any attention to your husband? Josephine, take care! Some fine night, the doors will be broken open, and there I'll be.

Indeed, I am very uneasy, my love, at receiving no news of you; write me quickly four pages, pages full of agreeable things which shall fill my heart with the pleasantest feelings.

I hope before long to crush you in my arms and cover you with a million kisses burning as though beneath the equator.

Bonaparte

The Hague, 1713

I am a prisoner here in the name of the King; they can take my life, but not the love I feel for you. Yes, my adorable mistress, tonight I shall see you, and if I had to put my head on the block to do it. For Heaven's sake, do not speak to me in such disastrous terms as you write; you must live and be cautious; beware of madame your mother as of your worst enemy. What do I say? Beware of everybody, trust no one; keep yourself in readiness, as soon as the moon is visible; I shall leave the hotel incognito, take a carriage or a chaise, we shall drive like the wind to Scheveningen; I shall take paper and ink with me; we shall write our letters.

If you love me, reassure yourself, and call all your strength and presence of mind to your aid; do not let your mother notice anything, try to have your picture, and be assured that the menace of the greatest tortures will not prevent me to serve you.

No, nothing has the power to part me from you; our love is based upon virtue, and will last as long as our lives. Adieu, there is nothing that I will not brave for your sake; you deserve much more than that. Adieu, my dear heart!

Arouet
[later known as Voltaire]

From George Washington to Mrs. Martha Washington

Philadelphia, June 18, 1775

*M*y dearest: I am now set down to write to you on a subject, which fills me with inexpressible concern, and this concern is greatly aggravated and increased, when I reflect upon the uneasiness I know it will give you. It has been determined in Congress, that the whole army raised for the defence of the American cause shall be put under my care, and that it is necessary for me to proceed immediately to Boston to take upon me the command of it.

You may believe me, my dear Patsy, when I assure you, in the most solemn manner that, so far from seeking this appointment, I have used every endeavor in my power to avoid it, not only from my unwillingness to part with you and the family, but from the consciousness of its being a trust too great for my capacity, and that I should enjoy more real happiness in one month with you at home, than I have the most distant prospect of finding abroad, if my stay were to be seven times seven years ...

As life is always uncertain, and common prudence dictates to every man the necessity of settling his temporal concerns, while it is in his power, and while the mind is calm and undisturbed, I have since I came to this place (for I

had not time to do it before I left home) got
Colonel Pendleton to draft a will for me, by the
directions I gave him, which will I now enclose.
The provision made for you in case of my death
will, I hope, be agreeable.

I shall add nothing more, as I have several letters to write, but to desire that you will remember
me to your friends, and to assure you that I am,
with the most unfeigned regard, my dear Patsy,
your affectionate, &c.

Wednesday, 13 October 1819
25 College Street

*M*y dearest girl,

This moment I have set myself to copy some verses out fair. I cannot proceed with any degree of content. I must write you a line or two and see if that will assist in dismissing you from my mind for ever so short a time. Upon my soul I can think of nothing else. The time is passed when I had power to advise and warn you against the unpromising morning of my life. My love has made me selfish. I cannot exist without you. I am forgetful of everything but seeing you again—my life seems to stop there—I see no further. You have absorbed me. I have a sensation at the present moment as though I was dissolving—I should be exquisitely miserable without the hope of soon seeing you. I should be afraid to separate myself far from you. My sweet Fanny, will your heart never change? My love, will it? I have no limit now to my love. Your note came in just here—I cannot be happier away from you. 'Tis richer than an argosy of pearls. Do not threat me even in jest. I have been astonished that men could die martyrs for religion—I have shuddered at it. I shudder no more—I could be martyred for my religion—Love is my religion—I could die for that. I could die for you. My creed is Love and you are its only tenet. You have ravished me away by a power I cannot resist; and yet I could resist till I saw you; and even since I have seen you I have endeavoured often "to reason against the reasons of my love". I can do that no more—the pain would be too great. My love is selfish. I cannot breathe without you.

Yours for ever,
John Keats

From Samuel Clemens, aka Mark Twain, to Mrs. Clemens

. . . Today I haven't a thing to report, except that I love you; that I love you and think of you all the time, and do immensely admire you—your mind as much as your person: your character and spirit far and away above these qualities as existent in any other person whom I have ever known. I am notorious, but you are great—that is the difference between us . . . You had a sentence in your letter that all the culture and all the genius and all the practice in the world could not improve. It was admirable. With all my heart.

Yours, Sam'l

Bologna, Aug. 25, 1819

*M*y dearest Teresa,—I have read this book in your garden. My love, you were absent, or else I could not have read it. It is a favourite book of yours, and the writer was a friend of mine. You will not understand these English words, and others will not understand them, which is the reason I have not scrawled them in Italian; but you will recognize the handwriting of him who passionately loved you, and you will divine that over a book which was yours he could only think of love. In that word, beautiful in all languages, but most so in yours,—*Amor mio,*—is comprised my existence here and hereafter. I feel I exist here, and I fear that I shall exist hereafter—to what purpose you will decide; my destiny rests with you, and you are a woman, eighteen years of age, and two out of a convent. I wish that you had stayed there, with all my heart—or, at least, that I had never met you in your married state.

But all this is too late. I love you and you love me,—at least, you say so and act as if you did so, which last is a great consolation in all events. But I more than you, and cannot cease to love you.

Think of me sometimes when the Alps and the ocean divide us; but they never will, unless you wish it.

Byron

From Robert Schumann to
Clara Wieck, who later became his wife

[c. September, 1837]

*D*ear and good Clara,—I have a request to make to you. Since now there is no electric current to draw us together, and remind us one of the other, I have hit upon the following joint plan—I shall play tomorrow, on the stroke of eleven, the adagio from Chopin's "Variations," and at the same time I shall concentrate my thoughts exclusively on you. Now you are please to do the same thing, so that we may meet and our spirits mingle. The meeting place of our "doubles" would probably be over the Thomaspfortchen. If there were a full moon, I should hold it up as the mirror of our letters. I am hoping for your answer. If you should not do this, and if a string should snap tomorrow in the twelfth hour—it would be myself. I speak with my whole heart.

Robert Schumann

London, May 8th, 1760

*M*y dear Kitty,—I have arrived here safe and sound, except for the hole in my heart, which you have made, like a dear, enchanting slut as you are.... And now, my dear, dear girl! let me assure you of the truest friendship for you, that ever man bore towards a woman. Where ever I am, my heart is warm towards you, and ever shall be till it is cold forever.

I thank you for the kind proof you gave me of your love and of your desire to make my heart easy, in ordering yourself to be denied to you know who; whilst I am so miserable to be separated from my dear, dear Kitty, it would have stabbed my soul to have thought such a fellow could have the liberty of coming near you. I therefore take this proof of your love and good principles most kindly, and have as much faith and dependence upon you in it as if I were at your elbow—would to God I was at it this moment! But I am sitting solitary and alone in my bed-chamber (ten o'clock at night after the play) and would give a guinea for the squeeze of your hand. I send my soul perpetually out to see what you are a-doing—wish I could send my body with it.

Adieu! dear and kind girl, and believe me ever your kind friend and most affectionate admirer. I go to the Oratorio this night. Adieu! Adieu!

P.S. My service to your Mamma.

Direct to me in the Pall Mall at the 2nd House from St. Alban's Street.

Royal Institution: Thursday evening
(c. December, 1820)

*M*y dear Sarah,—It is astonishing how much the state of the body influences the powers of the mind. I have been thinking all the morning of the very delightful and interesting letter I would send you this evening, and now I am so tired, and yet have so much to do, that my thoughts are quite giddy, and run round your image without any power of themselves to stop and admire it. I want to say a thousand kind and, believe me, heartfelt things to you, but am not master of words fit for the purpose; and still, as I ponder and think on you, chlorides, trials, oil, Davy, steel, miscellanea, mercury, and fifty other professional fancies swim before and drive me further and further into the quandry of stupidness.

From your affectionate
Michael

4/19/1908
2 Rivers, Wis.
9 p.m.

*J*ust had a five-mile hike—over sandy hills wild
and wind-beaten—and into pine woods along the
lake shore. Grand somber glooms under wide
branches, thickets & pools, & all the weird orches-
tration of frogs, crickets, night-birds, & whatnots
with tongues & throats & voices—A bog kept me
from reaching the shore—I could hear the
surge—it was like Freedom—"Ever beyond!" So I
took a seat (nobody asked me, Kitty, I wanted it
& just took it—that's the way with S-S!) yes, I
took a seat on a mossy, big log and lit a cigar. I
read out loud to the tintinabulation of the frogs
some lyrics to you. Some were original and some
not so original but they were all lyrics! I spoke
them to you—the "rythmic [sic] time of the
metronome of want" was in them—the Want of
YOU to be there—warm hand & wild hair and
good face—The shadows had come a-creepin',
slow and quiet but sure as shadows. The dusk
had fallen all around when I was getting the last
puffs on the cigar. I looked up at the sky and
startlingly near, thru the green-black boughs of a
massive pine was a burning, glowing star, a glitter-

---

ing, melting, concentrated flame seen thru this one hole in the roof of the forest. I called out to the Booger-Man, "You know the name o' that star?" "No," said the Booger-Man. "Well," I said, "you Ignorance! you, if anybody asks you, the name o' that star is *Paula!*" And the Booger-Man mumbled something and took hisself back where he come from. Wouldn't talk no more! Whatdye think o' that? The Duke sends love to the Duchess—gee! such a duchess!—and says to himself, "Hard lines" but is comforted with the Duchess saying, "God rest you, merry gentlemen!" adding sotto voce "sweet fool!" Wasn't that a trick of Fate to send your letters to Hartford when I'm in Two Rivers? I feel sorry for Fate—poor thing—using such a cheap stratagem to keep us from wigwagging our love-signals—Fate has a lot to learn yet!—

Good-night, Paula, my great-heart—like the pines and stars I worshipped with to-night—Good-night, Paula—I kiss your grand face—it's a night of grandeurs—and you are its star—Paula! I kiss you as the last glory of this night of glories.

Carl

July 23, 1914 New York
I had such a strangely beautiful dream last night, beloved Mary, and I want you to know it.

You and I were standing on a high green hill overlooking the sea, and you turned to me and said, "We must throw *her* back, Kahlil, we must throw her into the sea."

I knew you were speaking of a beautiful marble statue of Aphrodite that we had just unearthed—and I said: "But how can it be? She is so lovely. The rosy tint is still on her lips, and there is so much blue in her eyes."

Then you said, "But do you not see, Kahlil, that she would be much happier and more comfortable in the sea?" And I sadly said, "Yes."

Then we carried the large goddess as if she were a light thing—and from the top of a high white rock we threw her into the sea. And we were both glad.

Just then a flock of white birds flew before our eyes. And as they came near us they caught fire and were changed to flying flames. Then you said, "Do you not see I was right?" And I said, "Yes, you are always right."

Is not this a strange dream, beloved Mary?

Love from
Kahlil

From E.B. White, who signed himself
"Andy," to Katharine S. White

𝒟ear Katharine (very dear):

I've had moments of despair during the last week which have added years to my life and put many new thoughts in my head. Always, however, I have ended on a cheerful note of hope, based on the realization that you are the person to whom I return and that you are the recurrent phrase in my life. I realized that so strongly one day a couple of weeks ago when, after being away among people I wasn't sure of and in circumstances I had doubts about, I came back and walked into your office and saw how real and incontrovertible you seemed. I don't know whether you know just what I mean or whether you experience, ever, the same feeling; but what I mean is, that being with you is like walking on a very clear morning—definitely the sensation of belonging there.

This marriage is a terrible challenge: everyone wishing us well, and all with their tongues in their cheeks. What other people think, or wish, or prophesy, is not particularly important, except as it tends to work on our minds. I think you have the same intuitive hesitancy that I have—about pushing anything too hard, and the immediate problem surely is that we recognize & respect each other's identity. That I could assimilate Nancy overnight is obviously out of the question—or that she could me. In things like that we gain ground slowly. By and large, our respective families had probably best be kept in their respective places during the pumpkin weather—and gradually, like the Einstein drawing of Rea Irvin's, people will become accustomed to the idea that etc. etc.

I'm just writing this haphazard for no reason other than that I felt like writing you a letter before going to bed.

I love you. And that's a break.

Andy

From Dwight D. Eisenhower to Mamie Eisenhower

Algiers, January 4, 1943

I'm quite certain I've written you a dozen notes in the past few days, but you must put up with it because I get so much pleasure and relaxation out of picking up a pen and centering my thoughts exclusively upon you. All of us are torn this way and that—the days (and nights too) are just succeeding moments of turmoil, but I have the tremendous advantage in all this of knowing there is always you. So though my letters be poorly written and though they may be incoherent you'll realize that they just represent my instinctive turning to the one person in this world that will listen to me without criticism and with full understanding.

Lately I've heard much of you, indirectly. Everyone that comes from Washington tells me how well you look and how you're taking the war in your stride. It makes me extremely happy to hear such things. No one knows how much I want you to be happy—and when I get to thinking of all we (at least I) are losing by these months of separation, I do not like to feel that it is even worse than it need to be. I love you so very much that sometimes I wonder whether I've ever made you understand just how much it is. But then I remember that you've always figured me out so accurately that I quit worrying on that score.

The few American and British ladies here—
Red Cross, WAACS, nurses, employees and etc.
are all quite nice. . . . But the trouble is, darling,
that you're not among them. Sometimes I think
that if it were not for the ever present bombing
threat (when they come they're not so pleasant)
I'd be tempted to initiate a nefarious and unfair
scheme to get you here. If you were here—well,
why think of it. I'm old—my days of romance
may be all behind me—but I swear I think I miss
you more and love you more than I ever did.

"Come Live with Me, and Be My Love"

(Poems of Passion)

THE PASSIONATE SHEPHERD
TO HIS LOVE

Come live with me, and be my love,
And we will all the pleasures prove,
That valleys, groves, hills and fields,
Woods, or steepy mountain yields.

And we will sit upon the rocks,
Seeing the shepherds feed their flocks,
By shallow rivers, to whose falls
Melodious birds sing madrigals.

And I will make thee beds of roses,
And a thousand fragrant posies,
A cap of flowers, and a kirtle
Embroidered all with leaves of myrtle.

A gown made of the finest wool,
Which from our pretty lambs we pull,
Fair-lined slippers for the cold,
With buckles of the purest gold.

A belt of straw and ivy buds,
With coral clasps and amber studs;
And if these pleasures may thee move,
Come live with me, and be my love.

The shepherd's swain shall dance and sing
For thy delight each May-morning;
If these delights thy mind may move,
Then live with me, and be my love.

Christopher Marlowe

WESTERN WIND,
WHEN WILT THOU BLOW

Western wind, when wilt thou blow,
The small rain down can rain?
Christ, if my love were in my arms,
And I in my bed again!

Anonymous

MADRIGAL

My Love in her attire doth show her wit,
It doth so well become her;
For every season she hath dressings fit,
For winter, spring, and summer.
No beauty she doth miss
When all her robes are on;
But Beauty's self she is
When all her robes are gone.

Anonymous

TO CELIA

Drink to me only with thine eyes,
And I will pledge with mine;
Or leave a kiss but in the cup
And I'll not look for wine.
The thirst that from the soul doth rise
Doth ask a drink divine;
But might I of Jove's nectar sup,
I would not change for thine.

I set thee late a rosy wreath,
Not so much honouring thee
As giving it a hope that there
It could not withered be;
But thou thereon didst only breathe,
And sent'st it back to me;
Since when it grows, and smells, I swear,
Not of itself but thee!

Ben Johnson

SHE WALKS IN BEAUTY

She walks in beauty, like the night
Of cloudless climes and starry skies;
And all that's best of dark and bright
Meet in her aspect and her eyes:
Thus mellowed to that tender light
Which heaven to gaudy day denies.

One shade the more, one ray the less,
Had half impaired the nameless grace
Which waves in every raven tress,
Or softly lightens o'er her face;
Where thoughts serenely sweet express
How pure, how dear their dwelling place.

And on that cheek, and o'er that brow,
So soft, so calm, yet eloquent,
The smiles that win, the tints that glow,
But tell of days in goodness spent,
A mind at peace with all below,
A heart whose love is innocent!

Lord Byron

LOVE'S PHILOSOPHY

The fountains mingle with the river
    And the rivers with the Ocean,
The winds of Heaven mix for ever
    With a sweet emotion;
Nothing in the world is single;
    All things by a law divine
In one spirit meet and mingle.
    Why not I with thine?—

See the mountains kiss high Heaven
    And the waves clasp one another;
No sister-flower would be forgiven
    If it disdained its brother;
And the sunlight clasps the earth
    And the moonbeams kiss the sea:
What are all these kissings worth
    If thou kiss not me?

                   Percy Bysshe Shelley

UPON JULIA'S CLOTHES

Whenas in silks my Julia goes,
Then, then (methinks) how sweetly flows
That liquefaction of her clothes.

Next, when I cast mine eyes and see
That brave vibration each way free—
O how that glittering taketh me!

Robert Herrick

SHALL I COMPARE THEE
TO A SUMMER'S DAY?

Shall I compare thee to a summer's day?
Thou art more lovely and more temperate.
Rough winds do shake the darling buds of May,
And summer's lease hath all too short a date:
Sometime too hot the eye of heaven shines,
And often is his gold complexion dimm'd;
And every fair from fair some time declines,
By chance, or nature's changing course, untrimm'd;
But thy eternal summer shall not fade
Nor lose possession of that fair thou ow'st;
Nor shall death brag thou wand'rest in his shade,
When in eternal lines to time thou grow'st.
So long as men can breathe or eyes can see,
So long lives this, and this gives life to thee.

William Shakespeare

MEETING AT NIGHT

The grey sea and the long black land;
And the yellow half-moon large and low;
And the startled little waves that leap
In fiery ringlets from their sleep,
As I gain the cove with pushing prow,
And quench its speed i' the slushy sand.

Then a mile of warm sea-scented beach;
Three fields to cross till a farm appears;
A tap at the pane, the quick sharp scratch
And the blue spurt of a lighted match,
And a voice less loud, through its joys and fears,
Than the two hearts beating each to each!

Robert Browning

ON A GIRDLE

That which her slender waist confined
Shall now my joyful temples bind:
No monarch but would give his crown
His arms might do what this has done.

It was my Heaven's extremest sphere,
The pale which held that lovely deer:
My joy, my grief, my hope, my love
Did all within this circle move.

A narrow compass! and yet there
Dwelt all that's good, and all that's fair:
Give me but what this ribband bound,
Take all the rest the Sun goes round.

                              Edmund Waller

THE SONG OF SOLOMON

Behold, thou art fair, my love;
Behold, thou art fair;
thou hast doves' eyes within thy locks:
thy hair is as a flock of goats,
that appear from Mount Gilead.
Thy teeth are like a flock of sheep
that are even shorn,
which came up from the washing;
whereof every one bears twins,
and none is barren among them.

Thy lips are like a thread of scarlet,
and thy speech is comely:
thy temples are like a piece of a
pomegranate within thy locks.
Thy neck is like the tower of David
builded for an armory,
whereon there hang a thousand bucklers,
all shields of mighty men.
Thy two breasts are like two young
roes that are twins,
which feed among the lilies.
Until the day break,
and the shadows flee away,
I will get me to the mountain of
myrrh,
and to the hill of frankincense.
Thou art all fair, my love;
there is no spot in thee.

The Song of Solomon, 2:1—7.

More Love Stories— of Buttered Popcorn and Bicycle Tours

"With Pamela, it was her smell that got me. Buttered popcorn. Not lightly buttered either. This was in the days before there was such a thing as cholesterol. So buttered popcorn was actually considered to be a 'positive' food. Practically life-sustaining. Anyway, it was that smell that got to me. It seemed to envelop her, surround her, and make her both approachable and vulnerable.

"As someone who had spent most of his life inside an allergist's office, a non-allergenic scent was both welcome, and, ultimately, sexy. Flowers and perfumes only produced sneezes and wheezes. (In one memorable moment of my life, I had to ask my date to remove her angora sweater as I was having an asthma attack.) So, it was only natural that I would respond to a smell that was both attractive and non-rash producing.

"It's been twenty-five years now since I first encountered that scent. Amazingly enough, it hasn't gone away. So, in the morning, before she has a chance to put on her make-up or take a shower, I can smell that sweet vulnerability, that softness that made me fall in love with her in the first place."

Chuck, 49, advertising executive.
Married twenty-five years.

"The first time I saw the woman who would later become my wife, she breezed into a New York magazine office like some sort of apparition. I was in there pitching stories, before returning to Paris (where I lived at the time). Her boss had just suggested, 'Perhaps one of our editors will have some ideas for you.' In walked a woman with startling poise, independent demeanor, clad in a miniskirt. 'Sure,' she said, 'how about a story on . . .'

"Thus began our courtship, though it was hard to call it that at the time. Of course, I put an extra amount of energy into the story I wrote for her, but that wasn't the point. We had a reason to talk, and that we did. Over the following months, between Paris and New York, then between New York and San Francisco, our meetings seemed to be bracketed by phone conversations—though work was less and less what we talked about. There is definitely something to be said for the telephone as an instrument of love.

"Separated, but connected by the long wire of telecommunications, we jumped into subject matter—frivolous and serious, intimate, revealing, or hilarious—that we might never have gotten around to if we'd been physically together. That sexual charge, which was certainly there, had to wait for what soon became our regular cross-country meetings. We greeted each other in airports, we toured cities that neither of us knew. By the time we met in either of our hometowns, there was a bond that neither I, nor she, had been familiar with before.

"I fell in love with her wit, with her presence, her grace, and her vocabulary, her ability to mix words and sensuality. Often, her observations about people and events simply floored me. She seemed connected to the earth and yet willing to fly from it. We're different in some ways, but for that reason we build on each other's weaknesses, and support each other's strengths.

"But even if one were to thank the heavens for our meeting, at least some acknowledgment would still have to go to the telephone, to those unseen wires snaking under our streets, carrying passion, desire and intimacy like a long transcontinental fuse."

Mark, 37, free-lance journalist.
Married one and a half years.

"The first time I called her, I said, 'First you've got to say you won't hold this against me.'

" 'Hold what against you?' she said. 'Who is this?'

" 'First you've got to say you won't hold it against me.'

" 'Hold what?'

" 'That I broke Rule 16 of the Dating Code.'

" 'What's Rule 16?'

" 'Never to call a woman the day after you met her. It looks hopelessly uncool.'

"That's when, fortunately, she laughed.

" 'Forgive me?' I said.

" 'Yeah,' she said.

"That's when I told her who it was, though I think by that time she knew—we'd met at a party the night before—and we've been together ever since."

Jacob, 26, copywriter.
Going steady.

"For the longest time, I didn't even dare to make a move on Maria. She was the conductor, and I was just a pit musician, for this new Broadway musical. But when we were in Boston, on out-of-town tryouts, we'd sit up in her hotel room every night, talking and laughing and watching TV, until it was finally time for me to get up and go back to my own room—which was right next door. But even then, we'd ask each other, 'How long'll it be before you're washed up and in bed?' and then we'd call each other up on the house phone and talk for another hour. I was really going crazy, hearing her through the wall and knowing she was just a few feet away. But at the time we were both going out with other people, and we were supposed to be maintaining a professional relationship. While we were out of town, we managed to keep it up, but by the time the show got back to New York, we both knew that our other relationships were done for, and not long after that we moved in together. And ever since? We've been making beautiful music together."

Peter, 40, musician.
Married four years.

"It was 1975. We were on a bike trip, just the two of us, paralleling the Mississippi River from Wisconsin to New Orleans. I biked lead. Every time I'd glance in my rear-view mirror, there she'd be, in her bright orange helmet, pedalling along. Somewhere around St. Louis it occurred to me: I think this woman in the mirror likes me. By Vicksburg, I realized how in sync we'd become. By New Orleans, it was love."

Mark, 41, playwright and screenwriter.
Married fifteen years.

"The first date I had with Carol was almost my last. The whole thing was a comedy of errors. First, I was late picking her up because I got a ticket for making an illegal U-turn on the way to her apartment. Then, the restaurant had no record whatever of the reservation I'd made. Then, when we were done eating, I casually tossed my napkin onto the tabletop—where it immediately caught fire from the candle flame. I had to use the water from the ice bucket to put out the flames. When the whole thing was over, I was so mortified I didn't call her for a week—and I don't know if I ever would have had the nerve. But fortunately, she called me—and invited me over for dinner. I said, 'Are you sure you're willing to risk it?', and she said, 'No problem.' When I got there, she answered the door wearing one of those fireman's hats, and we both laughed. And I got through the whole evening without spilling, breaking, or setting fire to anything in her apartment. I was very pleased with my comeback."

Michael, 27, mortgage broker.
Currently "in love."

Proverbial Wisdom

*W*hat is a proverb, anyway? Is it not the distilled wisdom of the ages? A truth so profound and undeniable that anyone else—even from another culture, another land, another time—can hear it, smack his forehead, and immediately say, "Yep, they sure got that right"?

I think so.

And love and lust, matrimony and monogamy, have inspired a whole host of proverbs from around the world. Some of the best I've served up here, smorgasbord-style. So heap your plate high. And remember—however meaty these proverbs might be, they're essentially calorie-free. Reading them, you might put on wisdom, but never weight.

*M*arriage has teeth, and him bite very hot.

Jamaican proverb

*T*here is nothing better than a rich wife and a generous mother-in-law.

Russian proverb

A woman that loves to be at the window is like a bunch of grapes on the highway.

English proverb

*L*ove laughs at locksmiths.

American proverb

*M*attresses take care of marital spats.

Spanish proverb

A man builds the house, but a woman makes the home.

Jamaican proverb

A wife and a pot get better as they get older.

Japanese proverb

*W*hat a woman can carry in her lap, no man can carry in his cart.

Russian proverb

A fat wife is like a blanket in winter.

Pakistani proverb

A deaf husband and a blind wife are always a happy couple.

Danish proverb

*T*he goodness of a house does not consist in its lofty halls, but in its excluding the weather; the fitness of clothes does not consist in their costliness, but in their make and warmth; the use of food does not consist in its rarity, but in its satisfying the appetite; the excellence of a wife consists not in her beauty, but in her virtue.

Chinese proverb

A woman is flax, a man is fire, the devil comes and blows the bellows.

English proverb

*L*ove is a mousetrap—you go in when you wish, but you don't come out when you like.

Spanish proverb

$\mathcal{A}$ man without a wife is like a kitchen without a knife.

Jamaican proverb

$\mathcal{L}$ove and eggs must be fresh to be enjoyed.

Russian proverb

$\mathcal{M}$any court in poetry and after marriage live in prose.

American proverb

$\mathcal{A}$n old man in love is like a flower in winter.

Portuguese proverb

$\mathcal{I}$f young girls knew what old wives know, they would never marry.

Jamaican proverb

$\mathcal{L}$ove puts wings on your shoulders, but marriage puts crutches under your arms.

Russian proverb

$\mathcal{L}$ove lives in cottages as well as in courts.

English proverb

$\mathcal{L}$ove is a thing that sharpens all our wits.

Italian proverb

$\mathcal{A}$ man in love schemes more than a hundred lawyers.

Spanish proverb

$\mathcal{H}$usband and wife in perfect concord are like the music of the harp and lute.

Chinese proverb

$\mathcal{E}$ven a dog does not eat a marital quarrel.

Japanese proverb

$\mathcal{M}$ore belongs to marriage than four bare legs in a bed.

English proverb

$\mathcal{H}$ot love is soon cold.

American proverb

$\mathcal{I}$n bed—husband and wife; out of bed—guests.

Chinese proverb

$\mathcal{A}$ man without a wife is like a man in winter without a fur hat.

Russian proverb

As bad as marrying the devil's daughter and living with the old folks.

English proverb

The woman who dresses well draws her husband from another woman's door.

Spanish proverb

To tell a woman everything she may not do is to tell her what she can do.

Spain again

Early wed, early dead.

American proverb

If you want peace in the house, do what your wife wants.

African proverb

Don't blame your wife's side if your son is cockeyed.

Russian proverb

Though the husband be a flax-beater, his wife will call him to the threshold and sit with him.

Jewish proverb

A prudent wife is from the Lord.

Proverbs 19:14

Never marry a widow unless her first husband was hanged.

English proverb

The man who goes to bed to save his candle begets twins.

Chinese proverb

It is the beautiful bird which gets caged.

China again

Before you marry, keep your two eyes open; after you marry, shut one.

Jamaican proverb

Literary Love

$\mathcal{D}$id I ever tell you I won third prize in a short-story contest, sponsored by the Sons of Vespucci? No? I guess modesty is among my many virtues.

Still, I don't think even my prize-winning story would stack up to the stuff that follows. These are pretty heavyweight guys, writing about love and longing, about stolen kisses, secret trysts, and—believe it or not—even a romantic interlude at the dentist's office. (Is nothing sacred?)

Dig in. (And if, just for the record, you really *want* to see my Vespucci winner, I could probably find a copy for you.)

FROM . . . FOR WHOM THE BELL TOLLS
by Ernest Hemingway

*T*hen they were walking along the stream together and he said, "Maria, I love thee and thou art so lovely and so wonderful and so beautiful and it does such things to me to be with thee that I feel as though I wanted to die when I am loving thee."

"Oh," she said. "I die each time. Do you not die?"

"No. Almost. But did thee feel the earth move?"

"Yes. As I died. Put thy arm around me, please."

"No. I have thy hand. Thy hand is enough."

He looked at her and across the meadow where a hawk was hunting and the big afternoon clouds were coming now over the mountains.

"And it is not thus for thee with others?" Maria asked him, they now walking hand in hand,

"No. Truly."

"Thou hast loved many others."

"Some. But not as thee."

"And it was not thus? Truly?"

"It was a pleasure but it was not thus."

"And then the earth moved. The earth never moved before?"

"Nay. Truly never."

"Ay," she said. "And this we have for one day."

FROM ... *AFTER DARK, MY SWEET*
by Jim Thompson

*F*ay. She was coming out of the house, carrying a coffee tray. She was coming toward the garage, and she was dressed as she had been a few mornings ago—the day that Doc Goldman had called her and everything had started going to pieces.

Bare legs, bare shoulders, ivory-colored in the sunlight. Tan shorts, curved to the curves of her thighs; and the thin white blouse, drawn tight, straining softly with the flesh beneath it.

She saw me staring at her, and smiled. She paused beneath the window, looking up smiling. And if last night's whiskey had left any marks on her, I sure didn't notice. She looked just as fresh and beautiful as she had that other morning.

Her eyes were as sparkling and crystal clear as I remembered. Her hair had that same soft, brushed-shiny look, and, her face was the same rose-and-white softness.

Everything was the same. It was like that other morning all over again; as though it was still that morning and everything since then had been a bad dream.

"Well?" She smiled up at me. "Like to have some?"

I nodded. Or shook my head. Or something. I managed to mumble that I did.

"Some coffee, I mean?" she said.

And then she laughed and started toward the steps.

FROM ... *SISTER CARRIE*
by Theodore Dreiser

*C*arrie looked at him with the tenderness which virtue ever feels in its hope of reclaiming vice. How could such a man need reclaiming? His errors, what were they that she could correct? Small they must be where all was so fine. At worst they were gilded affairs, and ah, with what leniency are gilded errors ever viewed.

He put himself in such a lonely light that she was deeply moved.

"Is it that way," she mused.

He slipped his arm about her waist and she could not find the heart to draw away. With his free hand he seized upon her fingers. A breath of soft spring wind went bounding over the road, rolling some brown twigs of the previous autumn before it. The horse paced leisurely on, unguided.

"Tell me," he said softly, "that you love me."

Her eyes fell consciously.

"Own to it, dear," he said feelingly—"you do, don't you?"

She made no answer but he felt his victory.

"Tell me," he said richly, drawing her so close that their lips were near together. He pressed her hand warmly and then released it to touch her cheek.

"You do," he said, pressing his lips to her own.

For answer her lips replied.

"Now," he said joyously, his fine eyes ablaze, "you're my own girl, aren't you?"

By way of further conclusion her head lay softly upon his shoulder.

FROM ... *APPOINTMENT IN SAMARRA*
by John O'Hara

"One condition," he said.

"What?"

"Will you do it?" he said.

"I won't promise till I know what it is."

"That you be in bed when I get home."

"Now? In the afternoon?"

"You always used to love to in the daylight."
He reached over and put his hand high on the
inside of her leg.

She nodded slowly.

"Ah, you're my sweet girl," he said, already
grateful. "I love you more than tongue can
tell."

She spoke no more the rest of the way home,
not even goodbye when she got out of the car,
but he knew. It was always that way when they
were away from their home, and made a date to
go to bed when they got home. When they made
a date like that she thought of nothing else until
they got home. She wanted nothing else, and no
one else could take anything of her, not even the
energy that goes into gregarious gayety.... But
whenever they did that, from the moment she
agreed, to the ultimate thing, she began to submit.
And driving away he knew again, as he had
known again and again, that with Caroline that

was the only part of their love that was submission. She was as passionate and as curious, as experimental and joyful as ever he was. After four years she was still the only woman he wanted to wake up with ...

FROM ... *THE WAY OF ALL FLESH*
by Samuel Butler

*I*n money matters she was scrupulousness itself.
Theobald made her a quarterly allowance for her
dress, pocket money and little charities and presents. In these last items she was liberal in propor-
tion to her income; indeed she dressed with great
economy and gave away whatever was over in
presents or charity. Oh, what a comfort it was to
Theobald to reflect that he had a wife on whom
he could rely never to cost him a sixpence of un-
authorized expenditure! Letting alone her absolute
submission, the perfect coincidence of her opinion
with his own upon every subject and her constant
assurances to him that he was right in everything
which he took it into his head to say or do, what
a tower of strength to him was her exactness in
money matters! As years went by he became as
fond of his wife as it was in his nature to be of
any living thing, and applauded himself for having
stuck to his engagement—a piece of virtue of
which he was now reaping the reward.

FROM ... *THE GOOD SOLDIER*
by Ford Madox Ford

*A*nd now you understand that, having nothing
in the world to do—but nothing whatever!—I
fell into the habit of counting my footsteps. I
would walk with Florence to the baths. And, of
course, she entertained me with her conversation.
It was, as I have said, wonderful what she could
make conversation out of. She walked very lightly,
and her hair was very nicely done, and she dressed
beautifully and very expensively. Of course she
had money of her own, but I shouldn't have
minded. And yet you know I can't remember a
single one of her dresses. Or I can remember just
one, a very simple one of blue figured silk—a
Chinese pattern—very full in the skirts and
broadening out over the shoulders. And her hair
was copper-coloured, and the heels of her shoes
were exceedingly high, so that she tripped upon
the points of her toes. And when she came to the
door of the bathing place, and when it opened to
receive her, she would look back at me with a little coquettish smile, so that her cheek appeared to
be caressing her shoulder ...

Yes, that is how I most exactly remember her,
in that dress, in that hat, looking over her shoulder at me so that the eyes flashed very blue—
dark pebble blue ...

FROM ... *SWANN IN LOVE*
by Marcel Proust

*H*e ran his other hand upwards along Odette's
cheek; she gazed at him fixedly, with that lan-
guishing and solemn air which marks the women
of the Florentine master in whose faces he had
found a resemblance with hers. . . . She bent her
neck, as all their necks may be seen to bend, in
the pagan scenes as well as in the religious pic-
tures. And in an attitude that was doubtless habit-
ual to her, one which she knew to be appropriate
to such moments and was careful not to forget to
assume, she seemed to need all her strength to
hold her face back, as though some invisible force
were drawing it towards Swann's. And it was
Swann who, before she allowed it, as though in
spite of herself, to fall upon his lips, held it back
for a moment longer, at a little distance, between
his hands. He had wanted to leave time for his
mind to catch up with him, to recognize the
dream which it had so long cherished and to assist
at its realisation. . . . Perhaps, too, he was fixing
upon the face of an Odette not yet possessed, nor
even kissed by him, which he was seeing for the
last time, the comprehensive gaze with which, on
the day of his departure, a traveller hopes to bear
away with him in memory a landscape he is leaving forever.

FROM ... *THE BEAUTIFUL AND DAMNED*
by F. Scott Fitzgerald

On Thursday afternoon Gloria and Anthony had
tea together in the grill room at the Plaza. Her
fur-trimmed suit was gray—"because with gray
you *have* to wear a lot of paint," she explained—
and a small toque sat rakishly on her head, allow-
ing yellow ripples of hair to wave out in jaunty
glory. In the higher light it seemed to Anthony
that her personality was infinitely softer—she
seemed so young, scarcely eighteen; her form under the tight sheath, known then as a hobble-
skirt, was amazingly supple and slender, and her
hands neither "artistic" nor stubby, were small as
a child's hands should be.

As they entered, the orchestra were sounding
the preliminary whimpers to a maxixe, a tune full
of castanets and facile faintly languorous violin
harmonies, appropriate to the crowded winter grill
teeming with an excited college crowd, high-
spirited at the approach of the holidays. Carefully,
Gloria considered several locations, and rather to
Anthony's annoyance paraded him circuitously to
a table for two at the far side of the room.
Reaching it she again considered. Would she sit
on the right or on the left? Her beautiful eyes
and lips were very grave as she made her choice,

and Anthony thought again how naive was her every gesture; she took all the things of life for hers to choose from and apportion, as though she were continually picking out presents for herself from an inexhaustible counter.

FROM ... *McTEAGUE*
by Frank Norris

$\mathcal{A}$t two o'clock on Tuesdays, Thursdays, and
Saturdays Trina arrived and took her place in the
operating chair. While at his work, McTeague was
every minute obliged to bend closely over her; his
hands touched her face, her cheeks, her adorable
little chin; her lips pressed against his fingers. She
breathed warmly on his forehead and on his eye-
lids, while the odor of her hair, a charming femi-
nine perfume, sweet, heavy, enervating, came to his
nostrils, so penetrating, so delicious, that his flesh
pricked and tingled with it; a veritable sensation of
faintness passed over this huge, callous fellow,
with his enormous bones and corded muscles. He
drew a short breath through his nose; his jaws
suddenly gripped together vise-like.

But this was only at times—a strange, vexing
spasm, that subsided almost immediately. For the
most part, McTeague enjoyed the pleasure of
these sittings with Trina with a certain strong
calmness, blindly happy that she was there. This
poor crude dentist of Polk Street, stupid, ignorant,
vulgar, with his sham education and plebeian
tastes, whose only relaxations were to eat, to drink
steam beer, and to play upon his concertina, was
living through his first romance, his first idyl. It
was delightful. The long hours he passed alone

with Trina in the "Dental Parlors," silent, only for the scraping of the instruments and the purring of bud-burrs in the engine, in the foul atmosphere, overheated by the little stove and heavy with the smell of ether, creosote, and stale bedding, had all the charm of secret appointments and stolen meetings under the moon.

FROM . . . *TROPIC OF CANCER*
by Henry Miller

*I*t is to you, Tania, that I am singing. I wish that I could sing better, more melodiously, but then perhaps you would never have consented to listen to me. You have heard the others sing and they have left you cold. They sang too beautifully, or not beautifully enough.

It is the twenty-somethingth of October. I no longer keep track of the date. Would you say— my dream of the 14th November last? There are intervals, but they are between dreams, and there is no consciousness of them left. The world is a cancer eating itself away. . . . I am thinking that when the great silence descends upon all and everywhere music will at last triumph. When into the womb of time everything is again withdrawn chaos will be restored and chaos is the score upon which reality is written. You, Tania, are my chaos. It is why I sing. It is not even I, it is the world dying, shedding the skin of time. I am still alive, kicking in your womb, a reality to write upon.

FROM ... *COUPLES*
by John Updike

But it gave Piet pleasure to see Foxy, pregnant, reading a letter beside a wall of virgin plaster, her shadow subtly golden. And he wanted her to be pleased by his work. Each change he wrought established more firmly an essential propriety. At night, and in the long daytime hours when he was not yet with her, he envisioned her as protected and claimed by sentinels he had posted: steel columns standing slim and strong in the basement, plaster surfaces of a staring blankness, alert doors cleverly planed to hang lightly in old frames slumped from plumb, a resecured skylight, now of double thickness and freshly flashed, above her sleeping head. He saw her as always sleeping when he was not there, her long body latent, ripening in unconsciousness. Sometimes, when he came in midafternoon, she would be having a nap. The sea sparkled dark in the twisting channels. Lacetown lighthouse trembled in the distance and heat. High summer's hay smell lay thick upon the slope, full of goldenrod and field mice, down to the marsh. Beside the doorway there were lilac stumps. No workmen's cars were parked in the driveway, only her secondhand Plymouth station wagon, hymnal-blue.

FROM ... *THE POSTMAN ALWAYS RINGS TWICE*
by James M. Cain

I began to fool with her blouse, to bust the buttons, so she would look banged up. She was looking at me, and her eyes didn't look blue, they looked black. I could feel her breath coming fast. Then it stopped, and she leaned real close to me.

"Rip me! Rip me!"

I ripped her. I shoved my hand in her blouse and jerked. She was wide open, from her throat to her belly.

"You got that climbing out. You caught it in the door handle."

My voice sounded queer, like it was coming out of a tin phonograph.

"And this you don't know how you got."

I hauled off and hit her in the eye as hard as I could. She went down. She was right down there at my feet, her eyes shining, her breasts trembling, drawn up in tight points, and pointing right up at me. She was down there, and the breath was roaring in the back of my throat like I was some kind of a animal, and my tongue was all swelled up in my mouth, and blood pounding in it.

"Yes! Yes, Frank, yes!"

Next thing I knew, I was down there with her,

and we were staring in each other's eyes, and locked in each other's arms, and straining to get closer. Hell could have opened for me then, and it wouldn't have made any difference. I had to have her, if I hung for it.

I had her.

The Eternal Flame

(Ruminations on Commitment and Matrimony)

Marriage is like a pair of shears, so joined they cannot be separated; often moving in opposite directions, yet always punishing anyone who comes between them.

Sydney Smith (1771–1845)

When we consider what a young woman gives on her wedding day; she makes a surrender, an absolute surrender of her liberty, for the joint lives of the parties; she gives the husband the absolute right of causing her to live in what place, and in what manner, and in what society he pleases; she gives him the power to take from her, and to sue for his own purpose, all her goods, unless reserved by some legal instrument; and, above all, she surrenders to him her person. Then, when we consider the pains which they endure for us, and the large share of all the parental cares that fall to their lot; when we consider their devotion to us, and how unshaken their affection remains in our ailments, even the most tedious and disgusting; when we consider the offices they perform, and cheerfully perform, for us, when, were we left to one another, we should perish from neglect; when we consider their devotion to their children, how evidently they love them better, in numerous instances, than their own lives; when we consider these things, how can a just man think anything a trifle that affects their happiness?

William Cobbett Advice to Young Men (1762–1835)

*T*he chain of wedlock is so heavy that it takes two to carry it—sometimes three.

Alexandre Dumas

$\mathcal{I}$n Lapland friends are employed as negotiators with the girl's parents. Brandy is an essential requisite in these bitter climates, and supplied with plenty of this, the lover with his friends advances to the hut of the young woman's father, but he is not suffered to enter till the liquor is drunk, over which they discuss the proposals ... Every time he visits his intended bride, a bottle of brandy must be presented as a perquisite to the father, on which account the Wedding is often protracted for a year or two.

Marriage Rites, Customs and Ceremonies
by A.H. (1824)

$\mathcal{A}$ll husbands are alike, but they have different faces so you can tell them apart.

Anonymous

$\mathcal{A}$ handsome woman is a jewel; a good woman is a treasure.

Saadi

$\mathcal{N}$o man can either live piously or die righteous without a wife.

Jean Paul Richter

*H*appy and thrice happy are they who enjoy
an uninterrupted union, and whose love,
unbroken by any complaints, shall not
dissolve until the last day.

Horace

*I*f thou wouldst marry wisely, marry thine equal.
Ovid

*H*eaven will be no heaven to me if I do not
meet my wife there.

Andrew Jackson

*W*ives are young men's mistresses, companions
for middle age, and old men's nurses.

Francis Bacon
Of Marriage and Single Life

*T*o have and to hold from this day forward,
for better, for worse, for richer, for poorer,
in sickness, and in health, to love and to
cherish, till death do us part.

Book of Common Prayer

Matrimony,—the high sea for which no compass has yet been invented.

Heinrich Heine

To those brave men and women who have ventured, or intend to venture, into that state which is "a blessing to a few, a curse to many, and a great uncertainty to all", this book is dedicated in admiration of their courage.

E.J. Hardy
How to Be Happy Though Married (1885)

Of all actions of a man's life, his marriage does least concern other people; yet of all actions of our life 'tis most meddled with by other people.

John Selden,
Table Talk (1689)

It is easy to pass a jest upon the worldliness of property, but be assured that the two pillars upon which God has founded the edifice of civilized society are, after all, property and marriage.

Rt. Rev. Charles Merrivale, D.D. (1873)

$\mathcal{M}$arriage is the mother of the world, and preserves kingdoms, and fills cities, and churches, and heaven itself. Celibate, like the fly in the heart of an apple, dwells in a perpetual sweetness, but sits alone, and is confined and dies in singularity; but Marriage, like the useful bee, builds a house and gathers sweetness from every flower, and labours and unites into societies and republics, and sends out colonies, and feeds the world with delicacies, and obeys their king, and keeps order, and exercises many virtues, and promotes the interest of mankind, and is the state of good things to which God hath designed the present constitution of the world.

Bishop Jeremy Taylor
The Marriage Ring (c.1650)

$\mathcal{M}$arriage is one long conversation, chequered by disputes.

Robert Louis Stevenson
Memories and Portraits

$\mathcal{A}$ man and his wife, if at all properly mated, aren't simply two people who occupy adjacent beds. They have built up something together, they have united to weave about them a web of moral, social, psychical facts. To people who are very wretched together that web becomes a mass of thongs and the sooner these thongs are cut the better. But where there are love and passion and reliance and that sense of permanence of which I have spoken, violence to any shred of that web is like a scalpel on a naked nerve.

Ludwig Lewisohn
Stephen Escott

$\mathcal{P}$ersonally, I should estimate that in not one percent even of romantic marriages are the husband and wife capable of *passion* for each other after three years. So brief is the violence of love! In perhaps thirty-three per cent passion settles down into a tranquil affection—which is ideal. In fifty percent it sinks into a sheer indifference, and one becomes used to one's wife or one's husband as to one's other habits. And in the remaining sixteen per cent it develops into dislike or detestation.

Arnold Bennett
Mental Efficiency

Marriage should war unceasingly against a monster that is the ruin of everything: the monster custom.

A husband should never address an angry word to his wife in the presence of a third party.
The more one criticizes, the less one loves.

Love is the poetry of the senses. It holds in its hand the destiny of all that is great in man and of all that appertains to his mind. Either it is sublime, or it does not exist at all. When it does exist, it exists for ever, and grows greater every day. Love such as this was called the son of heaven and earth by the ancients.

Balzac
Physiologie du Mariage

If the home is an experiment and a risky experiment, one can only say that life is always like that. We have to see to it that in this central experiment, on which our happiness so largely depends, all our finest qualities are mobilized. Even the smallest homes under the new conditions cannot be built to last with small minds and small hearts. Indeed the discipline of the home demands not only the best intellectual qualities that are available, but often involves—and in men as well as in women—a spiritual training fit to make sweeter and more generous saints than any cloister. The greater the freedom, the more complete the equality of husband and wife, the greater the possibilities of discipline and development.

Havelock Ellis
Little Essays of Love and Virtue

The essence of a good marriage is respect for each other's personality combined with that deep intimacy, physical, mental, and spiritual, which makes a serious love between man and woman the most fructifying of all human experiences.

Bertrand Russell
Marriage and Morals

Sleep is still most perfect, in spite of hygienists, when it is shared with a beloved. The warmth, the security and peace of soul, the utter comfort from the touch of the other, knits the sleep, so that it takes the body and soul completely in its healing.

D.H. Lawrence
Sons and Lovers

Between husband and wife there should be no question as to *meum* and *tuum*. All things should be in common between them, without any distinction or means of distinguishing.

Martin Luther
Table Talk

(In Ayrshire) when a young man wishes to pay his addresses to his sweetheart, instead of going to her father's and professing his passion, he goes to a public-house; and having let the landlady into the secret of his attachment, the object of his wishes is immediately sent for, who nearly never almost refuses to come. She is entertained with ale and whisky, or brandy, and marriage is concluded on.

Sir John Sinclair
Statistical Account of Scotland (1791–1799)

I have found it impossible to carry the heavy burden of responsibility and to discharge my duties as King as I would wish to do without the help and support of the woman I love.

Farewell broadcast after abdication,
December 11, 1936.
Duke of Windsor (King Edward VIII)

*B*oire, manger, et coucher ensemble,
C'est mariage ce me semble.

Old French legal axiom

*I*t is better to marry than to burn.

St. Paul

"My Wife's a Winsome Wee Thing..."

(Poems of Devotion)

MY WIFE'S A WINSOME WEE THING

She is a winsome wee thing,
She is a handsome wee thing,
She is a lo'esome wee thing,
This sweet wee wife o' mine.

I never saw a fairer,
I never lo'ed a dearer,
And neist my heart I'll wear her,
For fear my jewel tine.

She is a winsome wee thing,
She is a handsome wee thing,
She is a bonie wee thing,
This sweet wee wife o' mine.

The warld's wrack, we share o't,
The warstle and the care o't,
Wi' her I'll blithely bear it,
And think my lot divine.

Robert Burns

There is a lady sweet and kind,
Was never face so pleased my mind;
I did but see her passing by,
And yet I love her till I die.

Anonymous (c. 1570)

A DRINKING SONG

Wine comes in at the mouth
And love comes in at the eye;
That's all we shall know for truth
Before we grow old and die.
I lift the glass to my mouth.
I look at you, and I sigh.

William Butler Yeats

BELIEVE ME, IF ALL THOSE
ENDEARING YOUNG CHARMS

Believe me, if all those endearing young charms,
　　Which I gaze on so fondly today,
Were to change by tomorrow, and fleet in my arms,
　　Like fairy gifts fading away!
Thou wouldst still be ador'd at this moment
　　　　thou art,
　　Let thy loveliness fade as it will,
And, around the dear ruin, each wish of my heart
　　Would entwine itself verdantly still.

Thomas Moore
Irish Melodies (1807)

WEDDED LOVE

　　My bride,
My wife, my life. O we will walk this world,
Yoked in all exercise of noble end,
And so through those dark gates across the wild
That no man knows. Indeed I love thee: come,
Yield thyself up; my hopes and thine are one:
Accomplish thou my manhood and thyself;
Lay thy sweet hands in mine and trust to me!

Alfred, Lord Tennyson

———

117

THE UNFADING BEAUTY

He that loves a rosy cheek,
    Or a coral lip admires,
Or from star-like eyes doth seek
    Fuel to maintain his fires:
As old Time makes these decay,
So his flames must waste away.

But a smooth and steadfast mind,
    Gentle thoughts and calm desires
Hearts with equal love combined,
    Kindle never-dying fires.
Where these are not, I despise
Lovely cheeks or lips or eyes.

Thomas Carew

NEW YEAR'S EVE

There are only two things now,
The great black night scooped out
And this fireglow.

This fireglow, the core,
And we the two ripe pips
That are held in store.

Listen, the darkness rings
As it circulates round our fire.
Take off your things.

Your shoulders, your bruised throat!
Your breasts, your nakedness!
This fiery coat!

As the darkness flickers and dips,
As the firelight falls and leaps
From your feet to your lips!

D. H. Lawrence

Even More Love Stories—
Secret Dances and
Skipped Classes

"This was back in the old days, the days of acid rock, the Vietnam War, and the Flower Child generation. Holly and I were both seniors at California State University, and history majors to boot, but up until then we didn't know each other. We had two classes together that year— psychology and British history—and that's where we met.

"God, how I hated our British history instructor. I would have dropped the class entirely if Holly hadn't been in it—and as it was, I purposely skipped class every now and then just so I could call her up for the assignments. Pretty clever, huh?

"And if she hadn't been in psych, I probably wouldn't have shown up there either. The teacher lectured strictly from the book, which made the class instruction redundant, to say the least. Still, the fact that Holly was there made it bearable. (I'd like to say enjoyable, but even Holly wouldn't believe that.) Of course, we both did ace the course.

"Anyway, from just such humble beginnings began a love that grows today as steadily as my waistline. The music, the fads and the wars have come and gone, but our marriage remains a life-boat through the turbulent seas of life. I'd like to wax even more poetic here, but poetry was one course I didn't take in college—which is a lucky thing, because if I had, we might never have met."

Keith, 39, broadcast executive.
Married sixteen years.

"Anne said the night she really realized how much I loved her was right after I'd finished shouting at her in the kitchen.

"We'd only been living together a few weeks, and we'd gone grocery shopping. When we drove home, we couldn't find a parking place anywhere near the apartment, so we unloaded the bags and I carried them upstairs while Anne drove off to park the car. It was after dark, and she didn't come back for ten minutes, then twenty, then a half hour. I really started to panic, and I left the house to go looking for her. I was really getting worried. When I came back again almost an hour later, all ready to call the cops, she was upstairs making a pitcher of iced tea and wondering where I'd been. When I exploded and asked her where on earth *she'd* been all that time—I found out later she'd bumped into an old girlfriend on the street—she just let me go on ranting and raving, and then said 'Geez, you really do love me, don't you?'

" 'Yeah, of course I do,' I told her. 'Why else would I be this supremely ticked off?' "

Gary, 27, hospital supplies salesman.

"To my mind, the acquisition of a wife is much like acquiring a sports car. Most important in the selection process are compatibility, comfort, and a nice shine. As time moves on, 'she' appreciates more and more rapidly, until you can't imagine how you've traveled life's roads without her. And in traveling some of the bumpiest roads, she manages to see you to your destination smoothly. Although men can often be quite demanding, our wives, like that fine sports car, continue to move right along with us. Also, we're proud of her when we notice that heads turn and other people comment on what a beauty 'she' is. Because all these things are so important, I think I've got the best wife anyone could ask for. But there is one other trait which I've so far neglected to mention—and that's economy. My wife is very economical, which simultaneously explains two things—why I'm quite happy with her, and why I don't have the sports car."

David, 30, engineering student.
Married five years.

"If I tell you what I love best about Debbie, you'll probably think I'm kidding—and she'll probably kill me—but here goes anyway.

"Whenever she's alone and doesn't think there's anyone around to notice, like when she's straightening up our apartment, or fixing something complicated in the kitchen, she'll break into this funny little dance, kind of a shimmy, to some little tune she's got playing in her head. She bites her lower lip, and just sort of bops around while she's doing whatever she's doing, but if you walk in on her, or she thinks somebody's watching, she stops instantly. I've caught her at it a few times, and it cracks me up everytime I do."

Jack, 23, actor (temporarily waiting tables).
Living together.

"I proposed to Beth on Valentine's Day, so it'd always be easy to remember. She was the only woman I'd ever met that I wanted to marry, but for reasons I don't even now fully understand. I had just suddenly had this realization that this was the right woman. So I went to Tiffany's to decide what sort of ring I liked, then I asked a friend, who was a jeweler, to get it for me on 47th Street. On Valentine's Day I got down on my one good knee, in the palatial 9-by-12-foot living room of our apartment, and asked her to be mine forever. I gave her the diamond ring, which I figured would clinch the deal, and Beth hugged me. Then I kind of blanked out until about three months later, at the wedding, where I was saying 'I do.' "

Tom, 44, magazine editor.
Married ten months.

Author's Note

$\mathcal{F}$inally, no such book as this could be complete without at least a few words, from the author himself, about the one woman in his own life. And now that I'm sitting down to do this, I can see why all the other men I spoke to were so slow in complying.

What do you say? How much should you divulge? What will her reaction be? Do I need to talk to a lawyer first?

Last night, I figured out, to my own surprise, that Laurie and I have been together for over five years. I wouldn't have thought it. We still chase each other around the room (though I'm older now and much easier to catch), and we still thoroughly enjoy each other's company; in fact, we'd better—because we're both working at home now and this apartment, while it's very nice, isn't what

you'd call grand. I think it's a real testament to
the strength of our marriage that we're together
all day long, and we still have plenty of things to
say to each other; true, they're sometimes on the
order of "Can I borrow your floss?" or "Why
doesn't Rex Morgan just marry June, his nurse?"
but hey, it's still conversation. And how many
times have you seen that most terrifying sight of
all—a married couple sitting in a restaurant, each
of them staring silently off into space, nothing left
to say, and no energy left to say it?

Spooky.

With Laurie, I can always count on a happy
face in the morning—which I don't usually see
till noon, when, in order to get a jump on the
day, I fall out of bed—and a willing companion
for all the day's events. Getting the mail. Empty-
ing the waste baskets. Fixing sandwiches. It's a
busy life we lead ... but still, we always find time
for each other.

In Laurie, I found someone bright and beautiful, sweet, sensitive, understanding. I got very
lucky indeed. If I could make a wish for everyone
else who comes across this little book, it's that
they, too, might find a love as rich and fulfilling
as the one I did.

Just leave Laurie out of it.

Robert 40, writer/lion of café society.
Married two and a half years.

Acknowledgments

To thank everyone who made this book possible—from Shakespeare to Voltaire, Ovid to Hemingway—would be a long and difficult business. And anyway, they'd never know I did it.

But there are others—living, breathing individuals—whose contributions I do wish to acknowledge. For assistance in the foreign languages department, Marcella Munson, Carol Weston and John Kluempers. And for all-purpose encouragement and support, my editor, Julie Merberg, and old friend (not that she's old, you understand) Joelle Delbourgo. And finally, I'd like to thank all the real men, whose full names I promised to keep confidential, who contributed their "Love Stories." It wasn't always easy to get them to open up ... but it was always worth it.

Thanks, everybody.

Bibliography

Alexander, Peter, ed. *The Complete Works of Shakespeare*. London and Glasgow: William Collins Sons & Co., Ltd., 1958.

Aller, Simeon, ed. *The Russians Said It First*. Los Angeles: The Ward Ritchie Press, 1963.

Ash, Russell, and Brian Lake, eds. *Bizarre Books*. London: Macmillan London Limited, 1985.

Ausubel, Nathan, ed. *A Treasury of Jewish Humor*. New York: M. Evans and Company, 1951.

Beck, Emily Morison, ed. *Familiar Quotations by John Bartlett, Fourteenth Edition*. Boston: Little Brown and Company, 1968.

Bohn, Henry. *A Polyglot of Foreign Proverbs*. London: Henry G. Bohn Publishers, 1857.

Butler, Samuel. *The Way of All Flesh*. New York: Grosset and Dunlap.

Cain, James M. *The Postman Always Rings Twice*. New York: Alfred A. Knopf, 1969.

Cohen, A., ed. *Ancient Jewish Proverbs*. New York: E. P. Dutton and Company, 1911.

Commins, Saxe, ed. *Basic Writings of George Washington*. New York: Random House, 1948.

Copeland, Lewis, ed. *Popular Quotations for All Uses*. Garden City, N.Y.: Garden City Publishing Company Inc., 1942.

Devereux, G.R.M. *The Lover's Dictionary*. London: C. Arthur Pearson Ltd., 1903.

Dreiser, Theodore. *Sister Carrie*. New York: Penguin Books, 1985.

Eisenhower, John D., ed. *Letters to Mamie*. Garden City: N.Y.: Doubleday and Company, 1978.

Ferrell, Robert, ed. *Dear Bess: The Letters from Harry to Bess Truman, 1910–1959*. New York: W.W. Norton & Company, 1983.

Fitzgerald, F. Scott. *The Beautiful and Damned*. New York: Charles Scribner's Sons, 1922.

Ford, Ford Madox. *The Good Soldier*. New York: Vintage Books, 1955.

Gardiner, Stanley, ed. *Letters of John Keats*. London: University of London Press Ltd., 1965.

Guth, Dorothy Lobrano, ed. *Letters of E.B. White*. New York: Harper and Row, 1976.

Harvey, Sir Paul, ed. *The Oxford Dictionary of English Proverbs*. Oxford: Clarendon Press, 1948.

Hemingway, Ernest. *For Whom the Bell Tolls*. New York: Charles Scribner's Sons, 1940.

Heseltine, G.C., ed. *A Bouquet for a Bride*. London: Hollis and Carter Ltd., 1951.

Hilu, Virginia, ed. *Beloved Prophet: The Love Letters of Kahlil*

Gibran and Mary Haskell. New York: Alfred A. Knopf, 1981.

Karlin, Daniel, ed. *Robert Browning and Elizabeth Barrett: The Courtship Correspondence, 1845–1846.* Oxford: Clarendon Press, 1989.

Kin, David, ed. *A Dictionary of American Proverbs.* New York: Philosophical Library, 1955.

Labor, Earle, Robert Leitz, I. Milo Shepard, eds. *The Letters of Jack London.* Stanford: Stanford University Press, 1988.

Mabie, Hamilton Wright, ed. *A Book of Old English Love Songs.* New York: The Macmillan Company, 1897.

Marvin, Dwight Edwards. *The Antiquity of Proverbs.* New York and London: G.P. Putnam's, 1922.

Miller, Henry. *Tropic of Cancer.* New York: Grove Press, 1961.

Modlin, Charles, ed. *Sherwood Anderson's Love Letters to Eleanor Copenhaver Anderson.* Athens and London: The University of Georgia Press, 1989.

Murphy, Edward F., ed. *2,715 One-Line Quotations for Speakers, Writers and Raconteurs.* New York: Crown Publishers Inc., 1981.

Norris, Frank. *McTeague.* New York: Vintage Books, 1990.

O'Hara, John. *Appointment in Samarra.* New York: Random House, 1934.

Okada, Rokuo. *Japanese Proverbs and Proverbial Phrases.* Tokyo: Japan Travel Bureau, 1963.

Norman, Charles, ed. *Come Live With Me: Five Centuries of Romantic Poetry.* New York: David McKay Company Inc., 1966.

The Oxford Dictionary of Quotations. Third Edition. Oxford: Oxford University Press, 1979.

Page, Robin. *The Country Way of Love.* New York: Penguin Books, 1983.

Proust, Marcel. *Remembrance of Things Past.* Translated by C.K. Scott Moncrieff and Terence Kilmartin. New York: Random House, 1981.

Rovira, Luis Iscla. *Spanish Proverbs.* Lanham, Md.: University Press of America, 1984.

Sandburg, Margaret, ed. *The Poet and the Dream Girl: The Love Letters of Lilian Steichen and Carl Sandburg.* Urbana and Chicago: The University of Illinois Press, 1987.

Scarborough, William. *A Collection of Chinese Proverbs.* Shanghai: American Presbyterian Mission Press, 1875.

Sherman, Robert, ed. *World's Great Love Letters.* Cleveland and New York: The World Publishing Company, 1943.

Simpson, Colin. *Emma: The Life of Lady Hamilton.* London, The Bodley Head, 1983.

Stallworthy, Jon, ed. *The Penguin Book of Love Poetry.* London: Penguin Books Ltd., 1973.

Talmey, Bernard S. *Love: A Treatise on the Science of Sex-Attraction.* New York: Eugenics Publishing Company, Inc., 1919.

Thompson, Jim. *After Dark, My Sweet.* New York: Vintage/Black Lizard, 1990.

Updike, John. *Couples.* New York: Alfred A. Knopf, 1968.

Vivian, Percival, ed. *Poems of Marriage*. London: George Routledge and Sons, Ltd.

Watson, G. Llewellyn. *Jamaican Sayings*. Tallahassee, Fla.: Florida A & M University Press, 1991.

Yaffe, H., ed. *Homage to Hymen: An Anthology for the Affianced and Married*. London: Faber and Faber Ltd., 1940.